DG Pocket

D0834541

Augusto Cavadi

Mafia
explained to tourists

di girolamo
editore

© 2008, by Di Girolamo Crispino

di girolamo è un marchio della **LEPDG**

Corso Vittorio Emanuele, 32/34 - 91100 Trapani
Tel./Fax 0923 540339
www.digirolamoeditore.com
info@digirolamoeditore.com
ISBN 978-88-87778-31-1
Impaginazione & Design: Vittorio Maria Vecchi
Stampa: Arti Grafiche Corrao - Trapani

CARATTERISTICHE
Questo libro è composto in Century Schoolbook con corpo carattere 11; è stampato su carta Selena Avoriata da 120 gr/m^2 della Cartiera Burgo; le segnature sono piegate a sedicesimo - formato rifilato 13,5x20 cm - con legatura in brossura e cucitura a filo refe; copertina stampata su cartoncino R 400 MATT Satin della cartiera Burgo da 300 gr/m^2 - plastificata con finitura opaca.

Introduction

When you mention mafia, "The Godfather" movies will probably be the first thing to come to mind in most people. Although this highly romanticized, fictional view of the phenomenon makes for excellent entertainment, the real Mafia, and the socio-cultural and historical context in which it is embedded, is somewhat more complex. This short work attempts to describe some of the real, historical and cultural aspects of mafia from its beginnings over 150 years ago, up to the present day. It also looks at the interesting and equally complex issue of what can be done to definitely eliminate mafia. A short bibliography is also included for those who would like more in depth information on this subject.

I wish to thank Tiziano Ciccarello and Stefania Arcara for their precious help with the translation and revision of this text.

The use of this booklet

It often happens that sociologists, journalists or tourists want to meet a Sicilian to discuss the mafia phenomenon more thoroughly. In an hour or two, you can only mention some of the main points that define the problem. After this brief introduction, those who are really interested in understanding the mafia phenomenon, should read at least three or four significant books on the subject. In fact, prejudice and clichés about mafia are widespread in the minds of foreigners, but even more so in the minds of Italians. Surprisingly, also in the minds of the Sicilians themselves, even in those with a university degree or working in the social service.

In an attempt to avoid a negative first impression, perhaps other than the emotional impact that a violent story may provoke, I have written this small book in six languages which lists the most frequently asked questions and misconceptions about mafia and their possible answers.

When I have thought it appropriate, I have quoted passages from available books on the subject, whose bibliographical references (to books or films) I have provided at the end of the volume, for those who are interested in further reading. You will notice that many of the suggested books have been written by Umberto Santino or by other members of the Centro Siciliano di Documentazione "Giuseppe Impastato"[1]

1 Giuseppe Impastato – called by his family and friends "Peppino" –

(Sicilian Centre of Documentation "Giuseppe Impastato"). I feel indebted to them, for without their intellectual effort and ethical commitment, even I – a qualified high school teacher of philosophy, history and civic education – would have only a superficial knowledge of the mafia phenomenon, and this book would have never been written.

A. C.

lived in Cinisi (the town where the "Falcone –Borsellino" airport was built) . After breaking with the mafioso tradition of his family, he actively promoted, with a group of "compagni" ("comrades"), a cultural, political and social movement of civil revolt. He paid for this intelligent and courageous commitment to social reform with his life on 9th May, 1978. The tireless efforts of his family (above all, his mother Felicia, his brother Giovanni and sister-in-law Felicetta), his comrades, and of the Centro Siciliano di Documentazione "Giuseppe Impastato", ultimately prevailed. It took twenty years but the criminal court finally convicted the notorious mafia boss Gaetano Badalamenti who commissioned Giuseppe Impastato's murder. A successful film directed by Marco Tullio Giordana reveals Giuseppe Impastato's story. *Card 1* (see at the conclusion of this text) describes Peppino Impastato's character; *card 2* helps you to better understand the film dedicated to him; *card 3* briefly presents the Centro Siciliano di Documentazione [a regional Sicilian activist centre] dedicated to Giuseppe Impastato and to anti-mafia causes.

I

Mafia: what is it about?

"We have been in Sicily for some days now, and we have not been involved in shootings between rival gangs. However, in the past twenty years, some of our journalists reporting from your island, have been seen on television with camouflage uniforms and bullet-proof vests..."

It is not the first time that misunderstandings like the one above have occurred. Highschool students, for example, from both foreign countries and Italy, have refused to participate in exchange programmes in Palermo because their parents feared for their lives and thought their children might be killed in the streets. The actual risk of being involved in violent street crimes is highly hypothetical and practically nonexistent. As far as I remember, the only documented case of tourists who were victims – though indirectly – of mafia related violence in recent times was that of an Austrian couple who, in 1992, were travelling on the motorway outside Palermo: they were involved in a car accident when a massive explosion blowed up the cars of magistrate Giovanni Falcone and his escort, who were killed. Such devastating and overt acts of violence are not characteristic of mafia behaviour. Statistically, it would be more dangerous to visit cities like Madrid, London or New York, which have been targets of terrorist attacks, or other cities on the planet, where you can find yourself in a bank or supermarket robbery.

"Does this mean that the mafia does not use violence?"

It is obvious that violence is the main means used by mafia to pursue its goals. What is usually ignored is that the type of violence used by contemporary mafia is not that of the American Old West or of the nineteenth-century Southern Italian bandits.

Contemporary mafia maintains its control primarily through intimidation. The violent means it uses to achieve its purposes are acts such as the destruction of orchards and the killing of cattle. Homicide is regarded as a last resort, as an extreme solution when usual methods have failed. When this happens, it is also considered a weakness in their means of control. When the mafia exercises authoritative control over a community and its institutions, this is referred to as "pax mafiosa" (mafioso peace)[2] and is the preferred condition that the mafia strives to achieve.

"Violence is therefore a means, an instrument of the mafia, but what are the goals that are pursued?"

Like every association, the mafia gangs, "Cosa No-

2 The term Mafioso indicates a person who is part or adherent to the mafia's organization or mentality. Also used as an adjective to express what is "mafia-like".

stra"[3] being the largest and strongest among these, come together to pursue their goals. The two main goals are certainly *power* and *profit*.

Regarding power, the *mafiosi*, unlike common criminals, do not set themselves *against* the state and its apparatus. Rather, they aim to penetrate into the institutions in order to manage them in a private and political way. This is the main reason why the current definition of mafia as "anti-state" can be considered incorrect and misleading.

In order to obtain political power (for example by influencing the electors' vote) it is necessary to have a lot of money. After acquiring key positions in the public administration, such offices become in turn a source of illegitimate profits. At this point, the vicious circle is closed, or rather, it turns into a vortex that becomes progressively more invasive. Politics is polluted with money, and polluted politics poisons the economy.

Nevertheless – according to some researchers such as Letizia Paoli in her *Fratelli di mafia* – it is erroneous to associate the Western capitalistic mentality with Cosa Nostra or 'Ndrangheta (the name of the mafia organization in the Italian region of Calabria): "The growth of *contra legem (against the law)* entrepreneurial activities and the subsequent maximizing of profits today do not represent the main goal. The mafia gangs are neither economic enterprises (...) nor industries of private protection. They share the same

3 Cosa Nostra is the name of the main mafia organization in Sicily.

symbolic, ritual and normative apparatus, and a single collective identity, and, above all, they aim at the exercise of political power within their own community".

"We are beginning to understand that the mafia is an organization whose goals of power and money are achieved through violent means. But then again, that is not much different from other organizations, more or less secret, in the rest of the world, whose members, disguised with good manners, forcefully defend their own interests violating ethics and the law."

Actually, there are many similarities between mafia gangs and other forms of organized crime. They are all are built more or less on the same model as the *'Ndrangheta* in Calabria, the *Camorra* in Campania, the *Sacra Corona Unita* in Puglia, the American *Cosa Nostra*, the Chinese *Triads* and the *Yakuza* in Japan as well as other criminal associations that are active in Central and South America, in Eastern Europe and Central Africa. Historically, mafia as we know it today emerged with the formation of the Italian Unitary State in 1861 and it adopted its structures, rituals and symbols from pre-existing secret societies such as the *Massoneria (Freemasons)*. If we look at geography, an aspect that should not be ignored is the fact that Sicilian bands did not just sporadically grow: they systematically expanded and have always entertained relationships, exchanges and conflicts with delinquents of every kind (from small local gangs to groups of unsuspected white collar criminals, like some Masonic lodges that are more or less notorious to the public) who, without scruples, try to acquire control over the institutions and the economy.

Despite the similarities, some specific features of mafia, especially the Sicilian mafia, exist. In fact, it wants to control and be rich with the broadest *consensus* possible. In order to achieve this in all social classes (farmers, urban working classes, as well as middle and upper-middle classes) the mafia uses — before and even more than intimidation — a sort of "social education". In other words, it passes on, from generation to generation, a *cultural code*: a set of values, beliefs, attitudes, prohibitions, and behaviours. This invests the mafia with a sort of moral legitimacy. The mafioso wants to be feared, but even more, he wants to be acknowledged, admired, honoured and respected. Without this essential component of social consent, an understanding of the mafia phenomenon would not be complete. Probably, it is precisely this old rooting in the territory that represents one of the characteristic features of mafia: *an archipelago of secret criminal organizations willing to conquer power and profit through violent strategies, but also through a subtle network of symbolic, ethical and relational complicity.*

II

Mafia: has it always existed?

"You mentioned that mafia – as we know it today – dates back to the second half of the 19th century. I suppose that it has not remained the same in the last one hundred and fifty years..."

As mafia opposes itself to some healthy parts of the State, but not to the State itself as an institution (which, on the contrary, it tends to colonise and exploit), it began to emerge in a definite form only when the small, single Italian states were united in the Sabaudo Kingdom, later Kingdom of Italy, in 1861. Before that date, historical records show a type of activities that Umberto Santino, in his book *La cosa e il nome*, calls "pre-mafioso".

The mafia has been able to survive for such a long time in a chameleon-like way: it has lived in a symbiotic relationship with the historical and social context, by adapting itself to its changes and updating some of its characteristics, but without losing its essential identity.

Studies done in the "Giuseppe Impastato" Centre describe three main phases of mafia's development: the *"agricultural* phase" (from the 1850s to the 1950s) that mainly involved the oppression of peasants and shepherds; the second *"urban-entrepreneurial* phase" (that entirely covers the 1960s) involving the government patronage, such as construction, contracts and real estate speculation; and the *"financial* phase" (from the 1970s to today) in which the profits from illegal activities, such as local protection money, arms and drug trafficking, are invested in international financial institutions with the help of expert financial advisors.

"But if this is the actual history, why do they speak about a 'good' mafia that was recently replaced by a 'bad' one?"

Here is another example of a mafia stereotype, a cliché which is both baseless and persistent. When, for example, a mafioso decides to collaborate with the magistrates (usually because he is pursued by his mafia enemies), or when, for example, lawyers defend people accused of mafia crimes – what commonly happens is that they invent this imaginary opposition between an "old" and a "new" mafia: the first respectful of the "values" (above all, honour), the second unscrupulous and unpredictable. Since the mafiosi live in the same social *environment* as all other Sicilians, they are subject to the same cultural changes of the period. Therefore also to the transition from one society, which is culturally more homogeneous and characterized by a more or less hypocritical religious morality, to a society that is fragmented, pluralistic and secular. Although social and historical changes have occurred, a mafia that is noble, chivalrous, loyal and protective of the weak, has never existed. The only mafia that ever existed has been characterized by betrayal among family and friends, delation to the police, killing of innocent witnesses including women, priests and even children. The only mafia that we know is primarily, if not exclusively, a parasite. It has never produced goods nor services (if we do not consider illegal products such as drugs). Instead, it has attacked and exploited people who were hard-working and full of initiative and who tried to build something positive for themselves and for those around them.

"When we watch television programmes on the mafia, we are tossed between two opposite images: mafia as only a Sicilian matter or on the contrary, mafia as a global empire that has its capital in Sicily and branches everywhere. Are both these images correct?"

Actually, both images are incorrect. Salvatore Lupo, a very competent historian, points out that it is wrong to think of "mafia as a local organization", but it is equally wrong to imagine mafia as "a monstruous animal based in Sicily whose tentacles reach out to the entire planet and that may obey to a single leader. You have to imagine mafia, on the contrary, as a network of business, family and urban relations and interests, that can be closely knitted over single territories such as a small town or a neighbourhood but can also cover larger areas such as the whole hinterland of Palermo.

Its extensions also link together environments that are completely different and geographically remote: the estates of Agrigento[4] and the citrus gardens of the *Conca D'Oro*[5], Little Italy and the docks of New York, areas where narcotics are produced and those where they are consumed. This network also includes criminals, businessmen, politicians, professionals: it connects the high and low places in society."

"In all these decades in Italy, different political regimes have followed. Has this been relevant for the development of mafia?"

Previously, I insisted on the cultural dimension of the mafioso system that would have been much less persistent in time if it had been only a mob of delinquents without ideas, without myths and without projects. However, the mafia's "world view" has never been rigid or crystallized once and for all, but it has strategically changed and adapted as necessary for its own ends. Politically, it is easier to describe what mafia *does not* tolerate, rather than what it tolerates: specifically a fair and unbiased legal system, uncorrupted by personal interests, a true and functional participatory democracy, the development of local and national economic resources, and the use of non-violence as a means of setting differences.

4 Like Palermo, Agrigento is another city and province of the Sicilian region.
5 The Conca D'Oro (Golden Valley) is a valley, just outside Palermo, famous for its numerous citrus orchards.

We know that the current mafia has emerged during the first decades of the Kingdom of Italy. Therefore it sought, and gained, the consent of important representatives of the monarchic-liberal regime. In the 1920s, when Fascism rose to power, it seemed that mafia had to succumb in front of an authoritarian government. What actually happened was that a large part of the unskilled labour mafia was imprisoned while many *leaders* reinvented themselves and integrated perfectly in the Fascist Party.

The role of the mafioso regarding the landing of the Americans in Sicily at the end of World War II has often been discussed, but the least that can be said is that prestigious exponents of "Cosa Nostra" were officially put in charge of a number of municipal administrations by the Allied troops. With the birth of the Italian Republic and with the approval of the current Italian Constitution, mafia did not get discouraged by the new atmosphere of freedom. On the contrary, as Giuseppe Carlo Marino writes in his *Storia della Mafia,* "it was elevated to the rank of a real political subject that, fearing the progress of the Italian Communist Party, became aware of its bargaining power, for the purposes of international interests of the so-called free world".

The mafiosi try to sense changes in direction of political tendencies in advance, for example, they were pro-Christian Democrat when the Christian Democrats held an absolute majority, pro-Socialist when it seemed that the scale was tipping towards a permissive Left Party, pro-Berlusconi when the nation's richest entrepreneur was able to found the most voted political party and be elected Prime Minister. In short, for the mafia, power does not have a political colour. If, for example, current trends of the "progressive" party and trade unions contrast with the established mafia cultural patrimony, this has not prevented in the past (and it won't in the future) that the mafiosi try to infiltrate into Left Wing organizations every time these have a chance to become the majority in the government.

"So far, you have spoken about the mafioso suggesting an all male organization. Does this mean that women never had an important role in mafia gangs?"

This is a delicate and problematic matter. As Anna Puglisi repeatedly stated in her book *Donne, mafia e antimafia*, it is necessary to start from proven information without being influenced by prejudice. Empirical observation tells us that in Sicily, as in the rest of the western world, women are emerging from a state of minority and subjection. Therefore it is not strange that this process of emancipation is reflected even within the mafia organizational structure. If it is true that "mafia is formally a male organization", it must be considered that "mafia male chauvinism is nothing less than the reflection of the male chauvinism of the social context and, since mafia does not have ideologies and its practices are characterized by a great opportunism, it is not surprising that it adjusts to a context in which women's role has become more important, apart from ethical evaluations on the contents and ways of practicing certain roles." We therefore see women who faithfully depart with their absconding husbands, who pass on mafia "values" to their children, who organize drug dealing or personally take part in it flying on long intercontinental trips, who replace their male relatives in leading the *clan*. Such female active participation has led to increasingly frequent cases of women in possession of mafia secrets who decide to "repent" (more or less sincerely), and to collaborate with the justice system.

In order to have a more complete view, Anna Puglisi reminds us of the increasing importance of women who are active "against" mafia. This includes women from different social classes who have come forward against mafia, for political and ethical reasons, or personal ones, such as the loss of relatives killed in mafia related crimes. As early as the end of the 19th century, many women were active in the peasants' struggles for the subdivision and assignment of large estates to farm workers. Particularly meaningful are the stories of those women who in the past fifty years took the sides of the State, against mafia, even if they came from mafia styled family traditions.

III

Mafia: will it always exist?

"Mafia is already a century and a half years old. Is it possible to predict its decline?"

Before being killed with his wife and his military escort in a bomb attack, Judge Giovanni Falcone made the following statement to the journalist Marcelle Padovani (in the book *Cose di Cosa Nostra*, now become a sort of moral testament): "For a long time we will still have to confront ourselves with the organized crime of the mafia. For a long time, but not forever: because mafia is a human phenomenon and as all human phenomena, it has a beginning, it undergoes an evolution, and therefore it will come to an end". The statement expresses a mix of realism because he admits that mafia, like a cancer, is hard to eliminate, and of optimism relying on the fact that there was a time when it did not exist, and it won't last for ever. Such belief obviously regards mafia as a specific social organization, and not as a symbol of delinquency in general. Wickedness and the will to dominate belong, even only potentially, to the genetic patrimony of humanity as we know from history. Just like goodness and the pleasure of friendly social organization also belong to it.

"Is it a matter only of passively waiting for the natural decline of mafia or also of actively working to accelerate it?"

To think that mafia is destined, like all historical forms, to dissolve does not mean having to tolerate it for who knows how long. It would be an absurd and paradoxical way to accept it by being excessively optimistic. It wouldn't be so different than to accept it for the opposite reasons, by being pessimistically certain that it cannot be eradicated.

It is a complex and many-sided matter, as previously noted, which requires an equally complex and organic solution. Sicilian individualism – probably not an exclusive feature of southern mentality, but certainly present in it – can be counted on by mafia as its strongest ally. It is difficult to imagine that people and organizations will put aside their pride, distrust and jealousies to work together for the common good, for a project that may be successful precisely because it is collective. This difficulty can help to explain what usually foreigners are rightly puzzled about: that is, how about five thousand "men of honour" can condition the freedom, employment, dignity and the same physical survival of about five million of their co-nationals. On the one hand, the five thousand belong, in fact, to *organized crime*: on the other hand, however, the five million do not allow themselves to be involved – firmly and permanently – in any *organized legality*. In fact, according to the testimony of Tommaso Buscetta – who was a controversial mafioso that collaborated with the justice system – those five thousand who belong to different mafioso "families" in practice can rely on a much wider circle of about one million people, who support mafia habitually or at least occasionally, out of personal interest or out of fear. Therefore five thousand are actively militant mafiosi; another million Sicilians are connected with the core of mafia organizations through more or less strong links: from the financial advisor to the chemist, from the local politician to the hospital head physician down to the local "pusher" and the *posteggiatore*[6]. What do the other four million people do? They essentially prefer to watch and wait for the outcome of the confrontation between mafia and the justice system, with the exception of a small but highly focused and active group of several thousand citizens who are involved, in various ways, in the "anti-mafia" movement. The above mentioned Judge Giovanni Falcone used the analogy of the Spanish *bullfight* to describe this uncertain situation: the crowd, representing the majority of the population, alternatively cheer for the *bull* (representing the mafia), or for the *bullfighter* (representing the criminal justice system), without really entering the arena and taking sides with one or the other.

---

6 A *posteggiatore* is a typical Southern Italian figure, often loosely connected with mafia, a sort of unauthorized parking valet who works in the streets of the city centre by demanding a fare for a public parking space that should be free; if the car owner refuses to pay, the car might be found "accidentally" damaged or even stolen.

"In actual fact, what overall strategy would be necessary to fight the mafia system?"

To begin with, what is needed is a major change in the way people think about mafia. This will require a massive educational effort starting from grade school through high school and university. But also the media, cultural associations and the Church should seriously make an effort in providing information on the subject. Usually, either the mafia problem is ignored, or it is discussed in a vague, folkloristic, or at least anachronistic way. The mafia's development should be more often a subject of serious study from a sociological, anthropological, psychological and historical perspective. Culturally, raising the population and legislature's awareness of the mafia activities is an important and necessary first step in bringing about a lasting social change. Additionally, the governing and opposing political parties also need to legislate and implement *self-regulatory laws* which should be strictly enforced, against the illicit practice of vote-buying and those who support mafia activities.

An essential element in a political system willing to undermine the mafia context would be the decision to to make the criminal justice system independent from the government. It would also be necessary to improve the professionalism and efficiency within the justice system, as well as within the police who collaborate with it. A *fast track* justice system which results in rapid trials and sentencing in civil and criminal matters would represent a significant tool in the prevention and repression of organized crime. Regarding this, the condition of the "witness collaborators" (citizens who freely testify against mafia criminals, contributing to their sentencing) and of the "justice collaborators" (inaccurately called *pentiti*, "repentants", by journalists) deserves particular attention. An improved and safer "witness protection programme", for these witnesses and their families is also very important. Both these categories of people, who are still underestimated, are crucial to the disruption of the mafia hegemony.

Culture, politics, justice: but also *ethics*. As previously observed, The mafia power system is embedded in a socio-cultural matrix: a way of thinking, a series of patterns of behaviours, of rules, and daily practices. All the educational bodies (families, schools, associations, political parties, trade unions, churches) must realize that, in the mafioso and *"mafiogenous"* social context, neutrality is illusive: either you overthrow the inspiring principles of the mafioso pedagogy (dogmatism, conformism, oligarchic structures, male chauvinism, privatization of power and of economic resources, contempt of employment...) or, by assuming a position of neutrality, you actually contribute to pass on these principles from one generation to the other. Some active members of the anti-mafia movement believe that Ghandi's non-violent philosophy and traditions might be the source of effective strategies, in the long term, in the education against mafia. This non-violent philosophy is represented in Sicilian history by the sociologist Danilo Dolci.

Economic reforms, finally, would complete the anti-mafia strategy. Appropriate and enforceable economic solutions would both cut off financing for mafia enterprises and increase public assets and services outside the mafia influence. Specifically, many changes are needed: strengthening the policies that support the anti-racket and anti-usury laws and associations, preventing the manipulation of public construction contracts (and subcontracts), effectively punishing unauthorized building through demolitions, suppressing financial speculation on waste recycling. Additionally, other forms of illicit mafia income such as cigarette contraband and drug trafficking need to be stopped. Facilitating legal immigration and fighting every form of human exploitation (including sexual exploitation of women and children). Also animal based sources of mafia income – the so called *"zoo-mafia"* – should be contrasted and not be underestimated, such as illegal horse racing, dog fighting and butchering. A more aggressive scrutinizing of banks regarding the source of incoming foreign capital, and the promotion of international agreements to close "tax havens", are also required at higher financial levels. Finally, a quicker redistribution of confiscated mafia assets needs to be favoured through legal reforms and when there are legal commercial products that derive from confiscated illegal assets, their circulation on the market should be made easier by – for example – the creation of a special trademark.

"Why is the Church also important in the process of reforming society to eliminate mafia?"

The history of Sicily cannot be considered separately from that of the Catholic Church. Sicilian history up to the present day has been influenced by religious institutions in general and by the Catholic Church in particular. It would be strange, then, if the deep penetration of Catholicism and mafia were independent phenomena.

An objective review of historical events, even recent ones, shows that there have been relationships between the mafia and the Catholic Church, with quite relevant consequences. There have been instances of actual complicity: priests and monks have been on friendly terms with mafia members, or they have been themselves directly involved in criminal activities such as extortion and blackmail. The archpriest of Caccamo[7], monsignor Panzeca, was known to host mafia *"summit"* meetings in his Church's rectory. He was considered to count more than his own brother, nominally the mafia boss in that area. On the other hand, there have been examples of priests who have been victims of mafia because they sided with the farm labourers or worked against mafia interests in socially depressed environments. One of these priests was Don Pino Puglisi, whose story is told by Umberto Santino in his *Storia del movimento antimafia* (*History of the Antimafia Movement*), a history that runs parallel to that of mafia for one and a half century. The image of Don Pino Puglisi as a priest and a friend is still vivid for us today. They killed him in 1994 in order to stop his education-

---

7 Caccamo is a small town, in the province of Palermo.

al and religious activities in one of the poorest and most criminally active neighborhoods in Palermo.

Priests martyred by mafia or complicit with it, however, are more the exception than the rule. In general, there has been a disenchanted indifference about mafia in the Christian Churches and in the Catholic one in particular, who unjustly considered it to be a matter for the government to deal with. The basis for this indifference was clearly summarised by Don Francesco Michele Stabile in an interview[8]. He explains that the Church hierarchies were extremely anxious about defending themselves from "ideological" enemies (such as masons, protestants and communists) and they have underestimated the moral and social pollution caused by illegal power systems. This is why "the mafiosi – who actually endangered the very root of the Christian Church – could be considered only as sinners to be rehabilitated, because they did not attack the Church on an ideological level, and on the contrary, they were among the promoters of religious and collective exteriors rituals. The mafia – as a criminal organization with its own culture and rituals – was not perceived as an obstacle to Christian evangelization". Instead, when direct relationships with the mafioso – or with politicians who were "friends" of the mafioso – could prove to be useful, bishops and clergy did not have any scruples.

The awareness of the mistakes that have been made in the past might help the Church to devote more attention to what Don Cosimo Scordato calls the "therapy for

8 I have republished the interview with Don Francesco Michele Stabile in my book *Gente Bella*.

a curable disease". In his precious book *Le formiche della storia*, he decribes two aspects of possible change (which he calls a "healing operation") on the part of the Church. He suggests that the Church can make changes that concern its own *internal* structure and somewhat authoritarian and dictatorial behaviour almost considered as mafioso. The elimination of the Church's pretension to moral superiority, a subsequent moral exclusion of certain individuals or groups, paternalistic, authoritative attitudes, lack of democratic decision and withdrawal of information. The Church should thus separate itself completely from existing political power and show itself to be interested more in the people's actual needs than in the affirmation of the Church itself. *Externally,* the Church should step forward and courageously exclude known mafia members, without preventing their return to the Church if this is done through a sincere and meaningful repentance for their prior criminal activities.

Further reading

Volumes

Those who would like to have a broader view on the different aspects of the mafioso phenomenon, will find the following books by Umberto Santino very useful: *Dalla mafia alle mafie. Scienze sociali e crimine organizzato*, Rubbettino, Soveria Mannelli (Catanzaro) 2006. The book is a guide to know the main studies on mafia. From the studies of sociologists, starting from the 1876 Franchetti report, to the more recent analyses of Arlacchi, Sciarrone, Paoli, Armao and others; from those of the historians, like Romano, Renda, Lupo, Marino, Dickie, to those of the economists, criminologists, psychologists and theologians. The last part of Santino's book is dedicated to the discussion of the "complexity paradigm" that has been adopted in the present work as a main interpretative key.

If you want to have a first, but reliable, knowledge of the history of the phenomenon, you can read *Storia della Mafia* (Newton Compton, Rome 1999), by Giuseppe Carlo Marino. He dedicates several pages to "the problem of the origins". Whoever wants to study this in depth can read Umberto Santino's *La cosa e il nome. Materiali per lo studio dei fenomeni premafiosi*, (Rubbettino, Soveria Monnelli [Catanzaro] 2000). The recent historical reconstruction by John

Dickie, *Cosa Nostra. A History of the Sicilian Mafia* (Hodder & Stoughton, London 2004), translated into Italian as *Cosa Nostra. Una storia della mafia siciliana* (Laterza, Roma - Bari 2005) manages to explain complex matters in a straightforward way. Giuseppe Carlo Marino evoked short biographies of some of the most notorious mafiosi in *I padrini. Da Vito Cascio Ferro a Lucky Luciano, da Calogero Vizzini a Stefano Bontate, fatti, segreti e testimonianze di Cosa Nostra...* (Newton Compton, Rome 2001).

In order to understand how Sicily is the home not only of the mafiosi but also of its most determined enemies, I suggest Luca Tescaroli's *Le voci dell'oblio. Il silenzio di coloro che non possono più parlare* (DG, Trapani 2005). In this volume, the author, who is also a judge, has collected his own articles from the Palermo edition of the newspaper "Repubblica". Those who would like to place mafia events and characters in a broader historical context are referred to Umberto Santino's comprehensive study *Storia del movimento anti-mafia* (Editori Riuniti, Rome 2004).

A detailed overview of mafia today can be found in Giovanni Falcone's interview with Marcelle Padovani *Cose di Cosa Nostra* (Rizzoli, Milan 1991). An updating of the "internal" organizational aspects and the "external" economic relationships can be found in Letizia Paoli's *Fratelli di mafia. Cosa Nostra e 'Ndrangheta* (Il Mulino, Bologna 2000).

Regarding the role of women "within" and "against" mafia, the collected essays by Anna Puglisi *Donne, mafia e antimafia* (DG, Trapani 2005) are instructive and easy to read. The same author published *Sole contro la mafia* (La Luna, Palermo 1990), the life stories of Michela Buscemi and Pietra Lo Verso, two courageous women from Palermo who, having relatives murdered, interrupted the chain of the mafioso revenge and testified against mafia in court. In *La mafia in casa mia* (La Luna, Palermo 1987, 2003) Felicia Bartolotta Impastato, Peppino's mother, tells her tormented and intense story to Anna Puglisi and Umberto Santino.

Regarding the difficult relationship between the Church and the mafia, in 1994, I tried to gather the most interesting contributions of historians, theologians, sociologists and witnesses in two anthological volumes *Il Vangelo e la lupara. Materiali su Chiese e mafia* (Dehoniane, Bologna) now unfortunately out of print. Waiting for these and other books that are also not available to be republished, one can consult pages 155-163 (with a bibliography on pages 180-182) of my book *Strappare una generazione alla mafia. Lineamenti di pedagogia alternativa* (DG, Trapani 2005); pages 239-258 of Cosimo Scordato's *Le formiche della storia. Un itinerario collettivo di liberazione all'Albergheria di Palermo* (Cittadella, Assisi 1994) and the book by various authors *Don Pino Puglisi. Prete e martire* (Il pozzo di Giacobbe, Trapani 1999).

The memory of the past is essential, but it is not enough. Honest Sicilians must do their part to overthrow the oppressive mantle of the mafia's domain. How? A very brief suggestion has been made in my 1993 booklet (revised edition 2004): *Liberarsi dal do-*

minio mafioso. Che cosa può fare ciascuno di noi qui e subito (Dehoniane, Bologna). In *Gente bella. Volti e storie da non dimenticare* (Il pozzo di Giacobbe, Trapani 2004), I then tried to evoke and give voice – using the "interview" style – to citizens more or less distinguished – teachers, sociologists, politicians, Catholic priests or Protestant ministers – who constantly work to build a different and better Sicily.

The references that I have made, incidentally, in the previous pages, to the usefulness of non-violence education (inspired by Ghandi and Dolci) are developed in the book written by various authors and edited by Vincenzo Sanfilippo, *Nonviolenza e mafia. Idee ed esperienze per un superamento del sistema mafioso* (DG, Trapani 2005).

Magazines

"Narcomafie" is the monthly magazine that, since 1992, the Abele Group of Turin has dedicated to topics such as legality, rights and citizenship. Through the web-site www.narcomafie.it it is possible to consult this magazine and subscribe to it.

"Limes", a bimonthly magazine of geopolitics by the publishing Group "L'Espresso", dedicated the issue number 2 of the year 2005 to the topic *Come mafia comanda.*

"Meridiana" dedicated several issues to mafia and anti-mafia.

Documentaries and other studies found in VHS, DVD and CD roms

Swiss-Italian Radiotelevision, *Intervista a Paolo Borsellino (Interview with Paolo Borsellino)*, 1992 (VHS); AA. VV., *La mafia. 150 years of history and stories*, Cliomedia Officina 1998, English translation 1999 (cd-rom); C. Lucarelli – G. Catamo, *La mattanza. Dal silenzio sulla mafia al silenzio della mafia*, Einaudi – Rai (book + DVD) 2004; S. M. Bianchi - A. Nerazzini, *La mafia è bianca*, BUR 2005 (book + DVD).

Films

The best monograph to this date on the subject is *La mafia nel cinema siciliano*, Barbieri, Mandria (Taranto) 2003, written by the film critic Vittorio Albano (1935 – 2003). Very interesting, too, by Michele Marangi and Paolo Rossi, *La mafia è cosa nostra - 10 film sull'onorata società*, Edizioni Gruppo Abele, Torino 1993. A rough distinction can be made between:

a) "Apologetic" films (that tend to represent a "mythical" mafia, that never really existed, based on honour and other traditional "values"): the well known F. Ford Coppola's series *The Godfather* (1972), followed by *The Godfather II* in 1974 and *The Godfather III* in 1990.

b) "Satirical" films (that use irony, often successfully, in order to demystify the apparent solemnity of mafia organizations): W. Allen, *Bullets on Broadway*, 1994 ; J. Huston, *Prizzi's Honor*, 1985; R. Benigni, *Johnny Stecchino*, 1991; R. Torre, *Tano da morire*, 1997.

c) "Socio-historical" films (that reconstruct historical or sociological stories): F. Rosi, *Salvatore Giuliano*, 1961; G. Ferrara, *Il sasso in bocca*, 1970; D. Damiani, *Confessioni di un commissario di polizia al Procuratore della Repubblica*, 1971; F. Rosi, *Il caso Mattei*, 1972; A. Di Robilant, *Il giudice ragazzino*, 1993; M. T. Giordana, *I cento passi*, 2000 (for further information on this film see below, Card 2); P. Scimeca, *Placido Rizzotto*, 2000; P. Benvenuti, *Segreti di Stato*, 2003; R. Faenza, *Alla luce del sole*, 2005.

d) "Literary films" (film adaptations of literary works): Elio Petri, *A ciascuno il suo*, 1967 (taken from L. Sciascia's novel with the same title); D. Damiani, *Il giorno della civetta*, 1968 (from L. Sciascia's novel with the same title). F. Rosi, *Cadaveri eccellenti*, 1976 (from L. Sciascia's novel *Il contesto*); E. Petri, *Todo modo*, 1976 (from L. Sciascia novel with the same title).

Web sites

www.centroimpastato.it (where you can find further information in foreign languages and references to other web sites).

Since 1995, about 800 groups and thousands of citizens have freely joined "Libera": at www.libera.it you can find documentation and updates. The files gathered in an anonymous dossier without a date,

Occhi aperti per costruire giustizia, were particularly useful for me, also to write this pamphlet.

Giuseppe Impastato: his activity, the murder, the investigations and the cover up

(by the Csd "G. Impastato")

Giuseppe (also known as Peppino) Impastato was born on 5th January 1948 in Cinisi in the province of Palermo, in a mafia family. His father Luigi had been sent into internal exile during the fascist regime, his unlce and his other relations were mafiosi, and his father's brother-in-law, Cesare Manzella, was a major mafia boss who was killed in a car bomb attack in 1963. While still a teen-ager, he broke off relations with his father – who kicked him out of the house – and initiated a series of political and cultural anti-mafia activities.

In 1965 he founded the newsletter *L'Idea socialista* and joined the left-wing PSIUP party. From 1968 onwards he took a leading role in the activities of the new revolutionary groups. He lead struggles by Cinisi peasants whose land had been expropriated to build the third runway at Palermo airport, as well as disputes involving building workers and the unemployed. In 1975 he set up *Music and Culture* with other young people in Cinisi, a group which organised debates, film, theatre and music shows. A self-financed radio station named *Radio Aut* was created in 1976, through which he exposed on a daily basis the crimes and dealings of *mafiosi* from Cinisi and Terrasini, principally the mafia boss Gaetano Badalamenti, who were playing a major role in international drug trafficking through their control of the nearby airport. The most popular programme was *Onda pazza* (*Crazy Waves*), a satirical broadcast in which he mocked politicians and *mafiosi*.

In 1978 he stood as a candidate in council elections for *Proletarian Democracy*, but was killed during the election campaign on the night between the 8th and the 9th of May, by a charge of TNT placed under his body, which had been stretched over the local railway line. (Two days later voters in Cinisi elected him as a councillor).

Initially the press, police and investigative magistrates talked about Giuseppe being a terrorist carrying a bomb, who caused his own death. Then, after the discovery of one of his letters written several months before his death, they started talking about suicide.

Thanks to the efforts of his brother Giovanni, his mother Felicia Bartolotta Impastato (who publicly broke off relations with their mafia relatives), his fellow activists and the *Centro Siciliano di Documentazione* (founded in Palermo in 1977 and named after Giuseppe Impastato in 1980), the mafia's responsibility for the crime was identified. And on the basis of all the evidence collected and the public accusations which were made, the case was reopened.

On 9th May 1979 the *Centro siciliano di documentazione* and *Proletarian Democracy* organised the first national demonstration against mafia in Italian history, in which 2,000 people came from all over the country.

In May 1984 the Court of Palermo issued a judgement (in line with the investigations carried out by Rocco Chinnici, a member of the first pool of anti-mafia investigative magistrates, who had been murdered in July 1983) confirming the mafia's responsibility for the crime, attributing it however to persons unknown.

In 1986 the *Centro Impastato* published a biography of Giuseppe's mother called *La mafia in casa mia*, and a dossier entitled *Notissimi ignoti* (*The Notorious Unknown*), in which Gaetano Badalamenti was identified as the instigator of the murder. Badalamenti, meanwhile, had been given a 45-year sentence for drug trafficking by a New York court in the 'Pizza Connection' trial.

In May 1992 the Court of Palermo, whilst recognising the mafia's responsibility for the murder, decided to end their investigations as they believed it impossible to identify the perpetrators. In May 1994 the *Centro Impastato*, supported by a sizeable petition, demanded the reopening of the case, and that a new supergrass from the Cinisi mafia named Salvatore Palazzolo be questioned for Impastato's murder. In March 1996 Giuseppe Impastato's brother and mother, and the *Centro Impastato*, presented a dossier in which they expressed the necessity to investigate the obscure events that took place - in particular the role of the *carabinieri* (police force) immediately after the crime.

Following a statement made by Salvatore Palazzolo, in which he named the boss Badalamenti and his second-in-chief Vito Palazzolo as the instigators of the murder, the investigation was formally reopened in June 1996, and in November the following year an arrest warrant was issued for Badalamenti.

In 1998 a committee was formed within Parliament's permanent anti-mafia commission to investigate the 'Impastato case'; and on 6th December 2000 it issued a report which outlined the responsibilities of State officials in leading the investigations astray.

On 5th March 2001 the Court of Assises declared Vito Palazzolo to be guilty of murder, handing down a thirty-year sentence. Gaetano Badalamenti was given a life sentence on 11th April 2002.

Bibliography on Giuseppe Impastato

Felicia Bartolotta Impastato, *La mafia in casa mia*, interview edited by Anna Puglisi and Umberto Santino, La Luna, Palermo 1986, 2000, 2003. Eu. 9.

Salvo Vitale, *Nel cuore dei coralli. Peppino Impastato una vita contro la mafia*, Rubbettino, Soveria Mannelli 1995, 2002. Eu. 15,50.

Umberto Santino (edited by), *L'assassinio e il depistaggio. Atti relativi all'omicidio di Giuseppe Impastato*, Centro Impastato, Palermo 1998. Eu. 20.

Peppino Impastato: anatomia di un depistaggio, The parliamentary anti-mafia report presented by

Giovanni Russo Spena, Editori Riuniti, Roma 2001. Eu. 9,30.

Giuseppe Impastato, *Lunga è la notte. Poesie, scritti, documenti* (edited by Umberto Santino), Centro Impastato, Palermo 2002, 2006. Eu. 8.

Anna Puglisi - Umberto Santino (edited by), *Cara Felicia. A Felicia Bartolotta Impastato*, Centro Impastato, Palermo 2005. Eu. 10.

"Peppino Impastato" Cultural Association, *Peppino Impastato: da Musica e Cultura alla Manifestazione Nazionale Antimafia*, Cinisi 2005. Eu. 3.

CARD 2

From the book *La mafia in casa mia* to the film *I cento passi*

The film *I cento passi* ("One Hundred Steps" – Italy 2000) has had the merit of reaching a larger audience, compared to the one we had reached before, to tell a story that, contrarily to what has been read and heard, is absolutely not marginal, of minor importance or dated. This story had already been told by Peppino Impastato's mother, Felicia Bartolotta, in a book published in 1986, *La mafia a casa mia*, where she narrates the relationship with her mafioso husband and her rebel son, speaking about her giving up the desire of revenge and affirming her right for justice even though it had been denied for many years. One of Peppino's companions, Salvo Vitale, has told the story in his book *Nel cuore dei coralli,* and so did journalist Claudio Fava in his book *Cinque delitti imperfetti,* Luciano Mirone in one of the chapters of his book *Gli insabbiati* and the many journalists who interviewed Peppino's mother, a woman always ready to tell her story and reveal what happened.

Twenty-two years of words and pictures, that certainly have not been able to reach as large an audience as that of a film awarded at Venice Film Festival. However, these words and pictures cannot be cancelled by the forgetfulness of those who have spoken of a "forgotten crime" and of "twenty years of silence". The film is intense and capturing and the Peppino Impastato character is played with intelligent identification, but, to be completely honest, not every aspect of the film convinced me. The metaphor of the "one hundred steps" (the distance between the Impastato's house and the house of Badalamenti) is suggestive, but the reality was more dramatic: Peppino had the mafia in his home and he had famous mafia bosses among his relatives such as Nick Impastato and Cesare Manzella, to whom Badalamenti seemed a rude parvenu ("He didn't even know how to clean his nose", says the mother in *La mafia in casa mia)*. The initial sequences of the film are inspired by conventional mafia imagery and there is a long harangue by Badalamenti who embodies the role of a life guide, although we then discover that the scene is only a nightmare of Peppino's: the attempt to "humanize" even a mafia boss appears a little over-done.

The scenes after the crime show how police major Subranni tried to prove that Peppino was only a terrorist suicide while Peppino's companions show a blood-stained rock proving that he had been killed or knocked down before being tied to the railway tracks. It wasn't only the carabinieri who tried to lead the investigations astray. Also the press tried to spread this disgraceful story with the exceptions of "Quotidiano dei Lavoratori" and "Lotta Continua". The film ends with the funeral and the red flags, a sort of deification of Peppino, but unfortunately the story did not really go this way. Youngsters were not present at the funeral, and there were very few fellow townsmen, and the majority of us who attended were from a different city. The final film credits report that the Public Prosecutor's office in Palermo has finally indicted Badalamenti after twenty long years for the murder of Giuseppe Impastato. Actually, the original draft of the film-script, in the final credit titles, mentioned that the Public Prosecutor's decision was taken "thanks to the effort of his family, of his companions and of the Impastato Centre", but this version was unexpectedly omitted. Without this effort that brought to important findings, to the forwarding of legal statements, dossiers and books – a unique case of people who collaborated with justice and spurred it into action – the investigation itself would have come to a standstill.

If the story of Impastato and his companions is emblematic of an era of heroism and struggle that represent the very best of 1968 and not a provincial version, we can also say that the story of the events after the crime was not less important. The fact that the mafia was not an archaic residue but was destined to grow and spread was sensed and understood only by few people. Therefore, the campaign launched, ten years before the anti-mafia laws, by the Palermo newspaper *Il Manifesto* for the "expropriation of mafia property", is worth more than many short-lived slogans from those years.

With the death of Impastato a new story begins, made of sidetracking, inertia, police and magistrature delays but also made of the great effort of his mother, brother, companions who still went strong (some of these knew they were risking a lot), and of us from the Sicilian Centre of Documentation, founded in 1977 and dedicated to Impastato precisely when many considered him an inexperienced and desperate terrorist. A year after the assassination, together with *Democrazia Proletaria* (Proletarian Democracy), we promoted a national demonstration against mafia that was the first in Italian history. At that point, to speak about mafia beyond the Sicilian limits was like conjuring up an unknown and impalpable ghost.

Nonetheless, two thousand people came from all over the country. As you can see going through the pages of the book in which we collected all the judicial acts (*L'assassinio e il depistaggio*), the investigations that had been hastily put aside were reopened, and then closed and reopened again several times, but finally these investigations came to conclusions that were unthinkable until a few years ago: on 5th March 2001 Badalamenti's vice, Vito Palazzolo, was condemned to thirty years of prison and Badalamenti himself was condemned to a lifetime sentence on 11th April 2002. In 1998, at the Centre's request, the Anti-Mafia Parliamentary Commission formed a committee on the "Impastato case" and on 6th December 2000, a report was officially issued clearly admitting that the representatives of the institutions (police and magistrature) had had a role in the sidetracking of the investigations. All of this was the result of daily efforts that joined with the good will of some magistrates like Costa, Chinnici, Caponnetto and Falcone, and a few others, who were willing to throw light on a truth that was and is uncomfortable. In the days after the funeral, Peppino's companions asked me to give the closing speech for the political campaign for the elections in which Peppino was candidate. I remember that the windows of the main street in Cinisi were closed and I decided to address my speech to those that hid behind the windows and were listening without being seen: "If these windows won't be opened, all of Impastato's efforts will be useless". Afterwards, there were the big crimes and massacres and a new awareness grew, but the processes of change are slow and they are not irreversible. Many windows, in Cinisi and elsewhere, have remained closed.

In the 70s, radical changes were thought possible and great expectations and strong hopes started to be nourished. Today, we have to deal with globalization that emphasises the gap between rich and poor countries, facilitates illegal accumulations on a worldwide scale and thus multiplies the mafias, as well as with the failure of the great perspectives of change. Nonetheless, Impastato's effort is still relevant today, as he was able to combine radical choices, starting with his decision to break up with his father, with the complexity of anti-mafia actions, carried out with documented and detailed reports to the police, social battles, cultural initiatives and with a continuous use of mockery and satire, that was considered by mafiosi a crime of lese-majesty.

"We'll still continue with Peppino's ideas and courage": this was written on a banner that opened Peppino's funeral. It is a hard and difficult commitment that has not always been kept. The film *I cento passi* recovers for today's audience a story that many wanted to forget but that instead remains among us and we have reasons to believe that it will continue to do so. The interest and emotion with which many, especially young people, see this film make us think that the efforts borne in these years, frequently carried out in great isolation, have given their fruits.

Umberto Santino

CARD 3

The Centro siciliano
di documentazionc
"Giuseppe Impastato": what it is
(by the Csd "G. Impastato")

The Sicilian Documentation Centre was the first centre for the study of mafia to be established in Italy. Founded in 1977 by Umberto Santino, it formally became a cultural association in May 1980 and was named after the New-Left militant Giuseppe Impastato, who was assassinated by the Mafia on 9th May 1978. Since 1998 the Centre is an "Onlus": "Non profitable and socially useful Organization".

The Centre aims at gathering knowledge about the mafia phenomenon and analogous phenomena, at a national and international level. Its purpose is to promote initiatives in order to fight such phenomena; to create and spread the culture of legality, development and democratic participation. Its activities are: gathering political, economic, historical and sociological materials; setting up study and research projects; promoting cultural initiatives (conferences, seminars, debates, exhibitions, etc.); publishing books, pamphlets and various material.

The Centre, which is completely self-financed, has built up a book and newspaper library and a specialist archive on mafia and other forms of organized crime. It has also produced studies and research projects, created bibliographies, run educational activities in schools and Universities in Italy and abroad. It has also promoted various initiatives towards mobilization (starting with the national demonstration against mafia, the first in Italian history, held in May 1979) and towards a wider social participation and had a crucial part in the investigation on the Impastato's murder.

With the research project «Mafia and Society», the Centre initiated a scientific analysis of the mafia phenomenon, carrying out researches on mafia murders in Palermo, on mafia-run businesses, on international narco-trafficking, on the relationship between mafia and politics and on the antimafia movement.

The Centre also collaborated with other associations for the planning of projects of social intervention and is engaged in the movement for peace, against the neo-liberal globalization and for the globalization of democracy and human rights.

Via Villa Sperlinga 15, 90144 Palermo
tel. 091.6259789
fax 091.348997
social security num.: 02446520823
e-mail: csdgi@tin.it
website: www.centroimpastato.it
c.o. box 1069090

Publications in English

U. Santino, *The financial mafia. The illegal accumulation of wealth and the financial-industrial complex*, in "Contemporary Crises", Vol. 12, No 3, September 1988, pp. 203-243, www.centroimpastato.it

U. Santino - G. La Fiura, *Behind Drugs. Survival economies, criminal enterprises, military operations, development projects,* Edizioni Gruppo Abele, Torino, 1993.

U. Santino, *The Law Enforcement against Mafia and Organized Crime in Italy and Europe*, in W.F. McDonald (editor), *Crime and Law Enforcement in the Global Village*, Anderson Publishing, Cincinnati, 1996, pp. 151-166, www.centroimpastato.it

U. Santino, *From the mafia to transnational crime*, in "Nuove Effemeridi", *Industry of violence*, Anno XIII, n. 50, 2000/II, pp. 92-101, www.centroimpastato.it

U. Santino, *Mafia and Mafia type organizations in Italy*, in J. S. Albanese, D. K. Das, A. Verma (editors), *Organized Crime. World Perspectives*, Prentice-Hall, Upper Saddle River, New Jersey, 2003, pp. 82-100, www.centroimpastato.it

Index

Notes

Notes

Notes

Notes

Notes

Notes

Notes